What Makes Me A
BUDDHIST?

Charles George

**KIDHAVEN
PRESS**™

San Diego • Detroit • New York • San Francisco • Cleveland
New Haven, Conn. • Waterville, Maine • London • Munich

© 2004 by KidHaven Press. KidHaven Press is an imprint of Thomson Gale, a part of the Thomson Corporation. Thomson is a trademark and Gale are registered trademarks used herein under license.

KidHaven™ and Thomson Learning™ are trademarks used herein under license.

For more information, contact
KidHaven Press
27500 Drake Rd.
Farmington Hills, MI 48331-3535
Or you can visit our Internet site at http://www.gale.com

LIBRARY OF CONGRESS CATALOGING-IN-PUBLICATION DATA

George, Charles 1949–
    Buddhist / by Charles George.
        p. cm. — (What makes me a—?)
    Includes bibliographical references (p.   ).
        ISBN 0-7377-2269-X
    1. Buddhism—Juvenile literature. [1. Buddhism.] I. Title. II. Series.
    BQ4032.G362   2004
    294.3—dc22

                                                    2003024344

Printed in the United States of America

CONTENTS

INTRODUCTION

A Religion or a Philosophy?

Today more than 400 million people around the world call themselves Buddhists. They follow the teachings of Buddhism's founder, Siddhartha Gautama, the Buddha. Even though most recognize it as one of the world's top four religions, is it truly a religion?

If the definition of a religion is "a system of beliefs in God or gods," then Buddhism does not qualify. Nowhere in the Buddha's teachings is a creator god mentioned. Most religions also teach that each individual has an eternal soul. The Buddha, however, felt this idea was an illusion—that we are all part of a single, universal "soul."

But, if religion is defined as the search for eternal truths to answer such questions as "Why am I here?" and "What is the meaning of life?" then Buddhism is a religion. Instead of focusing on God or the soul, Buddhism's goals are to get to know ourselves, so we can

More than 400 million people around the world practice Buddhism.

understand our true nature, and to learn about the Buddha's teachings. In that way, we can make our lives on Earth better and make the lives of those around us better. Whether Buddhism is a religion or a philosophy, people of all faiths can benefit from what Siddhartha Gautama had to say to the world so long ago.

CHAPTER ONE

How Did My Religion Begin?

Buddhism began more than twenty-five hundred years ago, when a young Hindu prince began teaching others in northern India what he had learned about life. His name was Siddhartha Gautama, but he came to be called the Buddha. *Buddha* is a title, meaning "the Enlightened One" or "the Awakened One." He received other titles as well—Bodhisattva, "a Being of Enlightenment," Shakyamuni, "Sage of the Shakya Clan," Tathagata, "the Thus-Perfected One," and Sugata, "the Happy One."

To enlighten is to teach or to give understanding. Someone who is enlightened is a person who deeply understands something. The Buddha understood the most important things there are—how to live a better life and how to be a better person.

Early Life

Siddhartha was born in about 566 B.C. near the foothills of the Himalayas, near the present-day border between India and Nepal. As a child, he was troubled with many of the thoughts and fears all children have. He wondered about birth and death. He struggled to understand why people got sick and what happened to people when they died. He wondered why his wishes did not always come true.

He was born into a very wealthy and powerful family. His father, Suddhodana, was a king, and his mother, Maya, a queen. Soon after Siddhartha was born, wise

Siddhartha, who came to be called the Buddha, was born in Nepal near the foothills of the Himalayas.

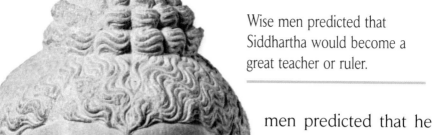

Wise men predicted that Siddhartha would become a great teacher or ruler.

men predicted that he would become either a great teacher or a great ruler, depending on what he learned during his childhood about the hardships of life.

Since his father wanted Siddhartha to inherit his kingdom and rule rather than teach, he decided to protect his son from the world until he inherited the kingdom. He kept his son in the palace for many years, isolated from the troubles of the real world, but Siddhartha eventually wanted to see the world beyond the palace walls.

Siddhartha Learns of Suffering

On trips outside the palace, Siddhartha saw things he did not understand—an old man, a sick man, a dead man, and a holy man. Because he had lived his whole life inside the palace walls, he had never seen illness, old age, or death, nor had he witnessed the suffering that goes with these events. He also had never seen anyone who gave up everything to seek the truth.

Siddhartha decided to try to find a way to relieve the suffering he saw. At age twenty-nine, he left the palace. He thought he could find the answer to unhappiness by giving up all of his possessions and joining a group of monks who traveled from town to town, begged for their food, and lived in the forest. Through feeling hunger, pain, and cold, he hoped to learn more about human suffering.

After six years of hardship and wandering, the answers Siddhartha looked for had not come. Nearly dead from starvation, his body almost a skeleton and

Siddhartha (in carriage) witnessed death on a trip outside the palace. Isolated for years behind palace walls, Siddhartha had never before seen death, illness, or suffering.

his skin black and shriveled, he decided to give up the homeless life and try to regain his strength.

Enlightenment

One morning in May, shortly after he made this decision, and thirty-five years since the day of his birth, a village girl brought him some rice boiled in cream and sweetened with honey. After eating the delicious rice, he bathed in the river and climbed up the bank to rest against the trunk of a large Bo tree, a type of fig tree, to rest. Somehow, he knew the time had come for him to find the answers he had been seeking.

Siddhartha vowed to sit under that tree, without food or water, and meditate, or think very deeply, until the answers came, even if it meant dying. He sat cross-legged for days and nights in deep meditation until he gained enlightenment. Finally, he realized that people suffered because they were never happy with what they had. They always craved more. He also saw a way out of this unhappiness. In all, he spent forty-nine days and nights meditating under what came to be called the Bodhi Tree, near present-day Bodh Gaya, India.

The Beginnings of Buddhism

After his enlightenment, he traveled to Deer Park, near the city of Benares, India, where he found the group of five monks he had joined years earlier. He taught them what he had learned, and they became his first disciples, or followers. This marked the beginning of Buddhism.

Buddha (left) teaches his disciples in this seventh-century carving. Buddha taught until his death at the age of eighty.

Over the next forty-five years, the Buddha walked from village to village in northeastern India, teaching and preaching to anyone who would listen. Many of those who understood what he was saying asked to join him and become Buddhist monks. He agreed and taught them how to teach others. By the time the Buddha died, at the age of eighty, hundreds of monks were spreading his message. Some eventually carried it to other countries in Asia.

As Buddhism spread, differences in the way the religion was practiced led to a split. Theravada Buddhism spread mostly to Southeast Asia, and Mahayana Buddhism spread to China and Japan. Two subdivisions of Mahayana have more recently risen to importance—Vajrayana, practiced in Tibet, and Zen, popular in Japan and the United States. Despite differences in practice, though, all followers believe in the essential truth of the Buddha's teachings.

CHAPTER TWO

What Do I Believe?

After his enlightenment, Siddhartha Gautama spread his message, or dharma, across India, teaching people of all social classes how to live a better life. Because of the depth of his message, many wondered if he was a god. At one point, he was asked this question directly, and he answered that he was not a god. Someone asked if he was an angel, and he said, "No." They asked if he was a saint, and he again said he was not. When they asked what he was, he answered, "I am awake."

Hindu Beginnings

What the Buddha meant was that he had become aware of the true nature of humans. His enlightenment, or awakening, revealed certain truths to him that are hidden from most people, and he spent the rest of his life sharing those truths. Much of what he said was

The Wheel of Dharma, seen here on the roof of a temple, is a symbol of the Buddha's message of how to achieve enlightenment.

new, but much came from the ancient religion of India—Hinduism. Siddhartha, after all, was born a Hindu.

Hindus believe in reincarnation, which means they believe people must live thousands of lifetimes—living, dying, and being reborn. Hindus also believe in karma, that people learn lessons each time they live on Earth, and that learning these lessons will eventually allow them to stop being incarnated and remain in the spirit world, nirvana. If a person does wholesome things and thinks wholesome thoughts, he will experience happiness. If he does not, he will experience suffering. This can also carry over into the next life.

Buddhism shares these beliefs with Hinduism, but with two major differences. Hindus believe a person is born into a certain caste, or social class, and must remain in that class. Buddhists believe in a classless society—that all people are equal. Another difference is reflected in the Buddha's teaching that a person can achieve nirvana in one lifetime, if he or she becomes enlightened. The heart of the Buddha's message is how to achieve enlightenment and is contained in the Four Noble Truths and the Eightfold Path.

The Four Noble Truths

The First Noble Truth is that life is full of unhappiness. No person can escape being unhappy at some point in life. This feeling of sadness could come from wanting something and not being able to have it. What the person desires might be a small thing, such as a child begging for a toy or game that his or her parent will not allow. It might be something major, like an orphan longing to be part of a loving family. This unhappiness could also come from having something, then losing it—a prized possession that is stolen or a loved one who dies.

The Second Noble Truth is that all suffering and unhappiness are the result of unsatisfied craving. Whatever a person receives, no matter how much or how good, never seems to be enough. People always want more, want something else, or want something to stop. It is human nature to continually want things we like and to not want things we do not like.

Buddhism students attend a discussion group. Buddha teaches that a person can achieve nirvana in one lifetime.

The Third Noble Truth is that the way to conquer suffering is to stop the constant craving. If a person can stop craving what he does not have, stop being envious of what other people have, and stop being so attached to what he already has, he will not suffer. This, however, is not easy. To accomplish this requires a great deal of effort and inner discipline.

The Fourth Noble Truth— the Eightfold Path

How to overcome craving is the subject of the Fourth Noble Truth. The Buddha taught that the way to conquer humankind's feelings of greed and desire is to follow a code of conduct that he called the Eightfold Path. This eight-step plan of action, if followed carefully, brings peace of mind and enlightenment. Sometimes called the Middle Path, the Buddha's eight steps include the following: Right Vision (or Understanding), Right Attitude, Right Speech, Right Action, Right Work, Right Effort, Right Mindfulness (or Awareness), and Right Meditation.

Right Vision means understanding the Buddha's teaching, particularly about who we really are. Buddhism teaches that we are not our physical bodies. Instead, we live in these bodies, but they are not our true selves. Our bodies will die, but we will not.

Right Attitude means we should think kind thoughts rather than cruel ones. We should try to think positively, not negatively. Kind thoughts build strong characters.

Right Speech, Right Action, and Right Work mean we should never say anything, do anything, or work in a job that harms any other person or animal. We should not tell lies, use angry words, or cause

A young Buddhist meditates to focus his thoughts and gain peace of mind.

anyone pain or embarrassment by what we say or do. Whatever we do for a living should not harm others or make others suffer. Speaking and acting honorably will bring honor, respect, and trust.

Right Effort means we should always think before we act. We should not act impulsively. Someone might suffer because of our actions. At the same time, we should be alert to what is going on around us and aware of our feelings. This is Right Mindfulness. Right Meditation means focusing on one thought at a time. By doing this, we can be calm and quiet. We can gain peace of mind.

The Five Precepts

Finally, to make his path clearer, the Buddha taught the Five Precepts—five simple rules of conduct that lead to a happy, peaceful life. Respect life; do no harm to living beings. Respect others' property; take nothing that is not freely given to you. Respect your pure nature; do not misuse your senses. Respect honesty; do not lie. Respect a clear mind; do not use drugs or alcohol because they cause a person to lose awareness. Following these simple lessons is not easy, but making the effort can lead to compassion, loving kindness, generosity, contentment, honesty, and learning.

The Buddha's lesson about never doing harm to another living being has led most Buddhists to be vegetarian. They do not eat meat, fish, or poultry because an animal would have to be killed. Many refuse to eat eggs because of the potential for life they contain.

Buddhist fathers teach their sons about the Five Precepts, simple rules of conduct that lead to a happy life.

Devout Buddhists, in addition to not eating meat, are careful not to harm even the smallest creature. A Buddhist will allow a mosquito to have a meal of his blood rather than swat it. Most offer prayers every morning asking forgiveness for any insect they might step on during the day. This becomes part of their everyday practice.

CHAPTER THREE

How Do I Practice My Faith?

To keep the Buddha's teachings fresh in their minds, Buddhists perform a variety of rituals. Some are daily practices, but others take place only on rare occasions.

Meditation and Prayer

Meditation is important for Buddhists. By training their minds, Buddhists can rise above their ordinary thoughts and bring themselves closer to enlightenment. Most meditate every day, seated cross-legged on the floor, but this is not a required position. A person can also meditate seated in a chair. The important thing is to be relaxed, to try to empty the mind of thoughts, and to focus on one thing, usually breathing. Some people find it helpful to focus on an object such as a flower or a candle's flame.

As in most religions, prayer is an important daily ritual. However, Buddhists prayers, like their meditations, are not intended to ask for anything or to beg forgiveness for a sin. Instead, Buddhists pray to remind themselves of lessons the Buddha taught. Some pray quietly, but others chant verses of the Buddha's teachings aloud. Some use a string of 108 prayer beads, called a *mala,* to help them concentrate. Prayer wheels, bells, and candles also aid them in their prayers. The acts of fingering beads, turning wheels, sounding bells, or lighting candles help them focus their thoughts.

Some Buddhists use a particular phrase in their prayers, repeating it over and over. This is called a mantra. Some use a single syllable that has no literal meaning. It merely serves as a way of concentrating the mind on one thing rather than letting other thoughts

Prayer is an important daily ritual in Buddhism. Buddhists pray to remind themselves of the Buddha's lessons.

intrude. Others meditate on the word *buddha.* One of the most popular and widely used mantras, however, is *om-mani-padme-hum.* This roughly translates as "jewel in the lotus" and refers to the purity of the Buddha's teaching.

Images and Offerings

Some people believe Buddhists bow to statues of the Buddha because they worship him as a god. This is not true. Buddhists bow to images of the Buddha out of respect for his teachings and as reminders that they, too, can gain enlightenment. They also bow to each other to show the same respect and reverence for life.

Buddhists sometimes place offerings before images of the Buddha, either in their homes, outside in peaceful settings, or in temples. These offerings, like their prayers, are meant to remind the person praying of some lesson he or she has learned, or to remind others of the lessons.

Many Buddhists light oil lamps, butter lamps, or candles because the Buddha's teaching is like a bright light to show the way to happiness. Some burn incense to show that, if the teachings are followed, people will be attracted to their goodness. Some leave flowers to show that humans are like flowers—of different shapes, colors, and sizes but all basically the same. Each of these offerings has one characteristic in common. They are impermanent, meaning they do not last. The lamps and candles burn out, the incense burns away, and the flowers wilt and fade. This illustrates the Buddhist principle

A woman offers burning incense to Buddha as she prays. Buddhist offerings are meant to remind the person of a lesson learned.

that nothing is permanent, and that we should not be attached to things.

Important Symbols

Buddhist temples contain images of the Buddha in various positions, standing, lying down, or seated cross-legged in the lotus position. The position of the Buddha's hands varies, too. These positions are called mudras, and each has a distinct meaning. Sometimes his hands are in the shape of an "O" to symbolize the continuity of life. Sometimes one hand will be raised in a gesture of protection and the other is open, palm forward, showing compassion. On

Buddha's hand positions have distinct meaning. Here, the raised right hand is a gesture of protection, while the open left hand shows compassion.

other statues, the Buddha's right hand touches the earth, so it can bear witness to his enlightenment.

Temple walls and religious objects also have other symbols significant for followers of the religion. The lotus flower is a powerful image for Buddhists. The roots of the lotus plant grow in mud and slime, but its flowers rise above the surface of the mud to bloom in the sunlight. Lotus leaves do not get wet. If water touches them, it runs off, just as evil does if the Buddha's teachings are followed.

The Cradle of Buddhism

Buddha was born in Lumbini in 566. B.C.

Buddha died at the age of eighty in Kusinara.

Himalayas

Delhi ✪

NEPAL

INDIA

Ganges River

Bodh Gaya

Buddha preached his first sermon in Sarmath.

Buddha achieved enlightenment in Bodh Gaya.

Indian Ocean

Other symbols are sometimes present in Buddhist shrines, but they vary according to country and culture. A common image is the Bodhi Tree, under which the Buddha attained enlightenment. Another is the dharma wheel, signifying the cycle of life, with its eight spokes symbolizing the Eightfold Path. In Tibetan Buddhist temples, monks often create sand mandalas, complex circular pictures made from loose multicolored sand.

Temples and Holy Sites

Buddhist temples are not places of worship, as churches, synagogues, and mosques are. Instead, they are places for meditation and contemplation. The first Buddhist shrines were dome-shaped buildings called stupas. The first eight of these were built in northern India and supposedly contain some of the Buddha's ashes, teeth, or bones. Today Buddhists meet in a variety of structures to learn more about the Buddha's dharma, including monasteries, shrines, dharma halls, and private homes.

Some Buddhists make pilgrimages to Buddhist holy places: Lumbini, where the Buddha was born; Bodh Gaya, where he experienced enlightenment; Sarnath, the site of Deer Park, where he first taught the Four Noble Truths; and Kusinara, the site of his death. For those who cannot make these pilgrimages, annual festivals are held to honor the life and teachings of the Buddha.

CHAPTER FOUR

What Holidays Do I Celebrate?

B uddhists are encouraged to consider every day, and every moment, special. Therefore, holidays are not occasions for special religious expression, as they are in Christianity, Islam, and Judaism. Holidays, for that reason, are less important in Buddhism than they are in other religions. Some Asian countries celebrate Buddhist holidays specific to their culture and traditions, such as honoring the life of a particular Buddhist teacher. Regular Buddhist holidays, celebrated in both Asia and the West, commemorate major events in the Buddha's life.

Wesak

The most important holiday of the Buddhist year takes place on the full moon of the sixth lunar month, usually in May but sometimes in June. This festival, called Buddha Day, or Wesak, celebrates three events in the

A Buddhist temple is decorated with prayer flags in honor of Wesak.

Buddha's life that supposedly happened on that date: his birth, his enlightenment, and his death. This is a joyful time of fellowship and study, usually marked with lively processions through the streets.

During Wesak, many followers renew their vows to follow the Buddha's teachings by chanting three short, significant phrases. This is called taking refuge in the Three Jewels. "I go to the Buddha for refuge. I go to the Dharma (teaching) for refuge. I go to the *Sangha* (the Buddhist community) for refuge."

Also during Wesak, followers clean their houses and streets and decorate with flowers, lanterns, and prayer flags, small colorful pieces of cloth with prayers written on them. They take offerings of food, candles, and flowers to monks and nuns in Buddhist monasteries and nunneries. Families also display images of the baby Siddhartha, with his hand pointing upward to truth. During Wesak, children greet their parents with gifts of flowers and send Wesak cards to friends.

Although most Buddhists celebrate Wesak in May or June, followers of the Zen school of Buddhism in Japan do not observe the holiday until December. In their celebration, they meditate and sometimes make a special effort to contribute time, labor, and money to a particular temple or monastery or to the community in general.

Dharma Day and Sangha Day

During the full moon in July, Buddhists worldwide celebrate a holiday that honors the Buddha's first sermon to the five monks in Deer Park. It is known as Asalha Puja, or Dharma Day. In October, another Buddhist holiday, Sangha Day, or Kathina Day, is celebrated. This festival coincides with the end of the monsoon, or rainy, season. Monks and nuns traditionally go on a three-month retreat during the rainy season. Sangha Day is a signal of its end. Villagers bring food, flowers, and new robes to the monks and nuns on this day each year.

Regional Festivals

Some branches of Buddhism observe holidays that other branches do not. On April 8, according to the Western calendar, Japanese Buddhists celebrate Hana Matsuri, an important Mahayana festival to honor the Buddha's birth. This day is usually devoted to children.

In some Buddhist schools, students wear flowers in their hair and perform a special ceremony, pouring water or scented tea over an image of the baby Buddha under a canopy of grass and flowers. They do this in memory of Buddha's first bath. According to Buddhist legend, when Buddha was born in a grove of trees, the earth shook and was flooded with light. The trees burst into bloom, and two streams of scented water, one hot and one cold, poured from the sky to wash him.

In Kandy, Sri Lanka, each year on the full moon of August, a magnificent procession of elephants passes huge crowds lining the streets. The largest elephant car-

A girl pours tea over a statue of the Buddha to celebrate Hana Matsuri, a festival that honors the Buddha's birth.

ries a small golden stupa containing a holy relic, said to be the Buddha's tooth. The festival also features dancers, drummers, and fire-eaters.

Followers of the Mahayana branch of Buddhism also celebrate a holiday in September called Ullambana. This holiday commemorates the action of Maudgalyayana, a disciple of the Buddha. Maudgalyayana's mother had been stingy and greedy in life, so her spirit was suffering. The Buddha told Maudgalyayana that he could make offerings to help release his mother and others from their suffering. This tradition of making offerings for dead ancestors continues during Ullambana.

In Thailand, Buddhists celebrate Loi Kratong, the Thai festival of light, on the night of the November full moon. When the moon rises, people gather on the riverbank and place lamps shaped like lotus flowers on the water. According to tradition, when the lamps float away, they carry bad luck with them.

Celebrating Milestones in Buddhist Life

Besides these annual festivals, Buddhists also celebrate special occasions in individual lives. Buddhist weddings are simple ceremonies, and even though a Buddhist monk may be invited, he does not take part in the ceremony. The couple stands on a special platform called a *purowa*, exchanges vows and rings, and has their hands loosely joined with a special silk scarf. After the ceremony, the family hosts a special feast.

Buddhist Celebrations Throughout the Year

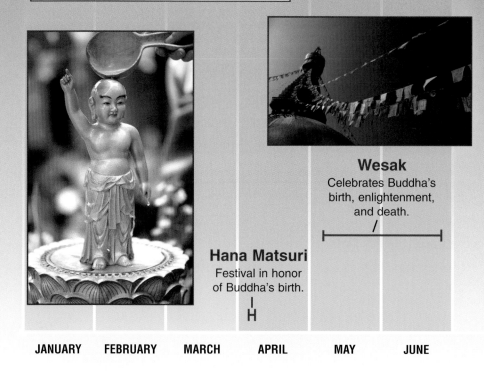

Wesak
Celebrates Buddha's birth, enlightenment, and death.

Hana Matsuri
Festival in honor of Buddha's birth.

JANUARY	FEBRUARY	MARCH	APRIL	MAY	JUNE

When a young Buddhist goes to a monastery, usually when the young man is about ten years old, there is a ceremony called an ordination. The young monk receives his robes and has his head shaved as a symbol of turning away from worldly things. In Thailand, his robe is orange yellow; in Myanmar and Tibet, maroon; and in Japan, black.

Buddhist funerals reflect the philosophy that nothing lasts forever and that everything changes. Even though sadness at the death of a loved one is natural, death is also considered a natural part of the life cycle. When a Buddhist dies, his or her family either buries or cremates the body, sometimes scattering the ashes in a

Dharma Day
Honors Buddha's first
sermon in Deer Park.

H

Ullambana
Commemorates the
actions of Buddha's
disciples.

Loi Kratong
Thai festival
of light.

Sangha Day
Celebrates the end of
the monsoon season.

H

JULY   AUGUST   SEPTEMBER   OCTOBER   NOVEMBER   DECEMBER

short ceremony. Monks conduct the ceremony and comfort the family. Later, friends and relatives offer gifts to monks, nuns, and to the poor to honor the departed.

Across the Buddhist world today, these festivals, along with personal ceremonies like daily prayers and meditations, remind Buddhists of the message taught so long ago by Siddhartha Gautama.

CHAPTER FIVE

My Religion Today and Tomorrow

In the two and a half centuries since the Buddha's death, his teachings have spread all over the world. Followers first carried his message out of India to west-central Asia and then east into China. From there, it spread to Korea and Japan; eventually southwest to Tibet, Nepal, and Bhutan; and southeast to Vietnam and Indonesia. Disciples also carried Buddhism from India southeast to what are now Sri Lanka, Cambodia, Myanmar, Thailand, and Laos. There is also evidence that Buddhist messengers traveled west to the Greek civilization in the eastern Mediterranean.

Buddhism Comes to the West

Until two hundred years ago, little was known about Buddhism in Europe and North America. During the mid-1800s some Western scholars began studying Buddhism and trying to translate Buddhist writings. In the United

States, authors like Ralph Waldo Emerson, Henry David Thoreau, and Walt Whitman became fascinated with the religion, and some of its ideas influenced their writing.

Widespread interest in the United States did not begin until 1893, when the World's Parliament of Religions was held at the Columbian Exposition, also known as the Chicago World's Fair. At that event, several Buddhist monks spoke, and people who listened to their speeches were impressed by the simple message they shared.

Buddhist Centers in the United States

During the twentieth century, and particularly after the 1950s, popular interest in Buddhism grew in the

Children attend an event at the Kurukulla Buddhist Center in Massachusetts.

United States. Asian immigrants had brought the religion with them, and some built retreat centers, monasteries, and *zendos,* or meditation halls, in locations across the country and in Canada and have opened their doors to the public.

The Naropa Institute in Boulder, Colorado, offers extensive academic courses in not only Buddhism but also other religious, spiritual, philosophical, and artistic subjects. The Chuang Yen Monastery in Kent, New York, has one of the finest Buddhist libraries outside of

More than five hundred Buddhist centers, like this one in Hawaii, now exist in the United States.

Asia. The monastery also features a thirty-seven-foot-tall statue of the Buddha, the largest in the Western Hemisphere.

Other popular Buddhist centers include the Zen Center of Los Angeles and the San Francisco Zen Center. At the Rocky Mountain Shambhala Center in Colorado, a magnificent stupa, the Great Stupa of Dharmakaya, has recently been completed. Spirit Rock Center in Marin County, California, and the Zen Mountain Monastery in Mount Tremper, New York, also offer Buddhist teaching and meditation. The Hsi Lai Temple, the largest Buddhist monastery in the Western Hemisphere, is in Hacienda Heights, California. In all, more than five hundred Buddhist centers now exist in the United States.

New Teachers, New Students

Americans' fascination with Buddhism has blossomed since the 1970s. Through books and lectures, Buddhist teachers like the Dalai Lama, head of the Tibetan branch of Buddhism, and Thich Nhat Hahn, a Zen monk from Vietnam, have sparked a lot of interest. Celebrities have also helped bring Buddhism to the country's attention. Actor Richard Gere, coach Phil Jackson, singer Bonnie Raitt, jazz musician Herbie Hancock, and movie director Oliver Stone are a few of the well-known students of Buddhism.

Magazine articles, books, television specials, and fea ture movies such as *Little Buddha* (1993), *Kundun* (1997), and *Seven Years in Tibet* (1997) have helped increase the

The teachings of the Dalai Lama, the head of the Tibetan branch of Buddhism, have sparked a lot of interest in Buddhism in the United States.

religion's popularity among the American public. Best-selling books about Buddhism appear on store shelves regularly. *Wherever You Go, There You Are,* by Jon Kabat-Zinn; *Awakening the Buddha Within,* by Lama Surya Das; *Being Peace,* by Thich Nhat Hahn; *Zen Mind, Beginner's Mind,* by Shunryu Suzuki; and *The Way to Freedom: Core Teachings of Tibetan Buddhism,* by the Dalai Lama are a few of thousands available.

Today Buddhism is the fourth-largest religion in the world. It has followers on every continent and is one of the fastest-growing religions in North America. In addition to the 400 million people who call themselves

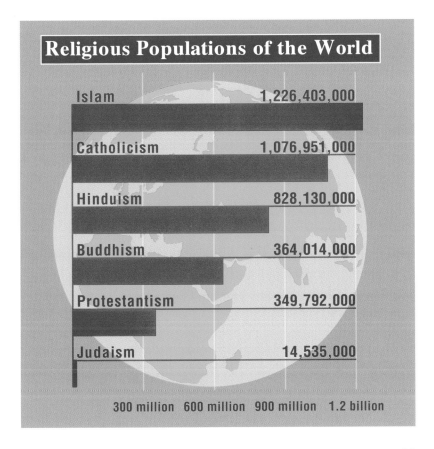

Religious Populations of the World

Islam	1,226,403,000
Catholicism	1,076,951,000
Hinduism	828,130,000
Buddhism	364,014,000
Protestantism	349,792,000
Judaism	14,535,000

300 million   600 million   900 million   1.2 billion

Buddhists, there are millions more who study its philosophy and apply elements of the Buddha's teachings to their own religions. In the United States today, there are ten times as many Buddhists as there were in 1960. At that rate of growth, there could be 15 to 20 million Buddhists by 2035.

Why Study Buddhism?

There are several theories for the rapid increase in interest in Buddhism in the United States and Canada. Some people are drawn to its simple message of peace and tolerance as a way of combating the violence they witness in the world. Others have lost interest in the religions of their childhoods because they see them as too judgmental and restrictive.

Some people are concerned about the condition of the earth and consider Buddhism's reverence for life a way to help preserve our environment. Others see how America's materialistic society is helping destroy our environment and are turning to Buddhism's simpler lifestyle. Some Christians and Jews feel comfortable accepting Buddhist ideas without abandoning their own faiths. They can do this because nothing in Buddhism conflicts or competes with Christian or Jewish religious beliefs.

Whatever the reason for the increase in interest in Buddhism in the West, and particularly in the United States, it is clear that the ideas taught by Siddhartha Gautama, the Buddha, more than twenty-five hundred years ago are having an impact on life today. Buddhism

New Yorkers gather in Central Park to discuss Buddhist philosophy. Today, people across the world are still drawn to Siddhartha's simple message of peace and tolerance.

seems simple, but explaining it to someone not familiar with its teachings and ideas is like trying to describe how an orange tastes to someone who has never tried one. You might be able to get the basic ideas across, like sweet, sticky, or juicy, but the only way to fully understand it is to taste one for yourself. Buddhism is difficult to explain. It must be experienced to be fully understood.

FOR FURTHER EXPLORATION

Books

Sherab Chodzin and Alexandra Kohn, *The Wisdom of the Crows and Other Buddhist Tales.* Berkeley, CA: Tricycle, 1998. Ranging from short Zen parables to longer folktales with dragons, goddesses, and talking animals, these tales explore Buddhist themes of compassion, humor, enlightenment, and life after death.

Hitz Demi, *Buddha.* New York: Henry Holt, 1996. A biography of the Buddha with exquisite illustrations and lovely, simple, descriptive language. It also includes several parables.

———, *The Dalai Lama: A Biography of the Tibetan Spiritual and Political Leader.* New York: Henry Holt, 1996. This book uses simple language and glorious art to pay tribute to the fourteenth Dalai Lama's life. It captures the beauty of the Tibetan culture.

Jill Foran, *Buddha Day.* Calgary, Alberta, Canada: Weigl, 2003. This work discusses how the celebration of

Wesak (Buddha Day) came about, what it signifies, and how it is celebrated.

Anita Ganeri, *Buddhist.* Danbury, CT: Childrens, 1997. This book introduces the religion of Buddhism, describing its origins and traditions. It includes related crafts and activities as well as a glossary and index.

———, *What Do We Know About Buddhism?* New York: Peter Bedrick Books, 1997. This book covers many aspects of Buddhism, including a biography of Siddhartha, the history of the religion, his basic teachings, and the religion's festivals and texts.

Jeanne M. Lee, *I Once Was a Monkey: Stories Buddha Told.* New York: Farrar, Straus, and Giroux, 1999. A retelling of six Jakata tales, fables told by the Buddha, which illustrate some of the central themes of the Buddha's teachings—compassion, honesty, and clear thinking before acting. It includes stunning illustrations.

Maura Shaw, *Thich Nhat Hahn: A Spiritual Biography for Young People.* Woodstock, VT: LongHill Partners, 2003. This biography emphasizes the spiritual beliefs that guided Hahn in trying to prevent war in Vietnam and have guided him in other political activism. It includes activities and a note for parents and teachers.

Philip Wilkinson, *Buddhism.* New York: DK, 2003. This book covers the history and practice of Buddhism, from the life of the Buddha to the religion's spread from Asia to the West. Beautiful photos show rituals, artifacts, and architecture.

Angela Wood, *Buddhist Temple*. Danbury, CT: Gareth Stevens/Franklin Watts, 1999. This work describes what happens in a Buddhist temple and introduces the faith. Vivid color photos and clearly written text explain the religion's basic beliefs and customs. It includes a glossary, index, and bibliography.

Web Sites

Bodhi Tales (www.bodhitales.org). A collection of Buddhist stories for children and adolescents that reflects the teachings of the Buddha.

Buddha Mind (www.buddhamind.info). An incredible Web site, full of state-of-the-art graphics, hidden links, codes, and games, all associated with the study of Buddhism. This site could be a little advanced for young children.

Buddhanet (www.buddhanet.net/mag_kids.html). The children's section of an online Buddhist magazine that includes interactive areas for making two pictures of the Buddha, a storybook about a young Buddhist monk and his friends, and a comic strip based on one of the Buddha's Jakata tales.

INDEX

PICTURE CREDITS

ABOUT THE AUTHOR

Charles George taught history and Spanish in Texas public schools for sixteen years. He now lives with his wife of thirty-three years, Linda, in the mountains of New Mexico. Together they have written more than forty young adult and children's nonfiction books. Charles has written two Lucent books, *Life Under the Jim Crow Laws* and *Civil Rights;* the KidHaven book, *The Holocaust,* part of the History of the World series; and *The Comanche* and *The Sioux,* for The North American Indians series. He and Linda also wrote *Texas,* for the series Seeds of a Nation.